Anonymus

A catechism of the history of England

Anonymus

A catechism of the history of England

ISBN/EAN: 9783741178658

Manufactured in Europe, USA, Canada, Australia, Japa

Cover: Foto ©ninafisch / pixelio.de

Manufactured and distributed by brebook publishing software
(www.brebook.com)

Anonymus

A catechism of the history of England

A CATECHISM

OF THE

HISTORY OF ENGLAND.

BY THE AUTHOR OF

"AN INTRODUCTION TO ENGLISH HISTORY," ETC.

LONDON:

BURNS, LAMBERT, & OATES, 17, 18 PORTMAN STREET,

AND 63 PATERNOSTER ROW.

CONTENTS.

CONTENTS.

A CATECHISM

HISTORY OF ENGLAND.

———◆———

CHAPTER I.

THE ANCIENT BRITONS.

Question. Who were the first inhabitants of Great Britain?

Answer. Great Britain is thought to have been first peopled by a colony of Celts from the neighbouring country of Gaul.

Q. What was the character of the ancient Britons?

A. They were a brave and warlike people, divided into tribes, each of which was ruled by its own chief. These tribes were for the most part fierce and barbarous; but in the southern part of the island they were more civilised.

Q. What do we know of their mode of life?

A. They had towns and villages formed of rude huts; they kept large herds of cattle, and in some parts tilled the ground and grew corn. Their dress was chiefly of skins, and the wilder tribes painted their bodies with the figures of flowers and animals.

Q. What was their religion?

A. Like the Gauls, they followed the religion taught by the Druids.

Q. Who were the Druids?

A. The Druids were the priests, who not only presided over affairs of religion, but also directed the laws and the education of youth.

Q. What was the religion they taught?

A. It was one of the worst forms of idolatry, including even human sacrifices. The oak and the mistletoe, as well as rocks and fountains, were objects of worship.

Q. From what time does our first acquaintance with Britain and its inhabitants commence?

A. From the year 55 before Christ, when the island was invaded by the famous Roman general, Julius Cæsar.

Q. Did he conquer the country?

A. After his first landing he was obliged to withdraw to Gaul; but returning the next year with a larger force, he crossed the Thames, defeated Cassibelaunus, the British chief, burnt his capital of Verulam, and laid the Britons under tribute.

Q. Who completed the conquest of Britain?

A. In the year A.D. 43 Claudius Cæsar, Emperor of Rome, again invaded the island. Four years later all the tribes south of the Tyne were conquered, and the brave King Caractacus was sent in chains to Rome.

Q. What British queen bravely opposed the Roman governor Suetonius?

A. Boadicea, Queen of the Iceni, who raised the eastern provinces in insurrection. She was at last defeated, and poisoned herself to escape captivity, A.D. 62.

Q. Who introduced the Roman civilisation into Britain?

A. Julius Agricola, appointed governor by the Emperor Vespasian. He likewise led an army into Caledonia, and constructed a fortified wall between the Friths of Clyde and Forth, to keep off the incursions of the Picts and Scots.

Q. What other walls were built by the Romans in Britain?

A. The Emperor Hadrian raised an earthen rampart from the Solway Frith to the Tyne. This was afterwards repaired by Severus, and formed the boundary of the Roman province.

Q. What Roman emperor was born in Britain?

A. Constantine the Great, the son of St. Helena. He was born at York.

Q. How long did the Romans remain in Britain?

A. Until the reign of the Emperor Honorius, A.D. 420, when the Roman legions were finally withdrawn from Britain.

Q. What followed on the withdrawal of the Romans?

A. The Britons suffered much from the renewed incursions of the Picts and Scots, and, after vainly appealing to the Romans for help, they at length called in the aid of the Saxons.

Q. Who were the Saxons?

A. The German tribes inhabiting the country to the north of the Rhine.

CHAPTER II.

THE BRITISH CHURCH.

Q. When and by whom was Christianity introduced into Britain?

A. It is uncertain at what precise period Christianity was first introduced; but it was probably in the second century after Christ.

Q. Who was the first British martyr?

A. St. Alban, who suffered at Verulam, in the persecution of Diocletian.

Q. What do we know of the early British Church?

A. We know that the early British Christians were in communion with Catholic Christendom; that they had monasteries and colleges; that they acknowledged the authority of the Holy See of St. Peter, and sent Bishops to the Councils of Nice, Arles, and Sardica.

Q. Mention some of the most famous British saints.

A. St. Alban, St. David, St. Winifred, and St. Ursula.

Q. What heresy made great ravages in Britain in the fifth century?

A. The heresy of Pelagius, who was himself a Briton by birth. St. Germanus, Bishop of Auxerre, twice visited this island to oppose the British Pelagians.

CHAPTER III.

THE SAXONS.

Q. What chiefs led the Saxons into Britain?

A. Two brothers, named Hengist and Horsa, A.D. 449.

Q. What followed on their arrival?

A. The Saxons, after defeating the Picts and Scots, turned their arms against the Britons, and soon made themselves masters of the country.

Q. What was the character of the Saxons?

A. They were fierce sea pirates, and professed a barbarous pagan worship.

Q. What became of the Britons?

A. Many were reduced to slavery by the Saxons; others took refuge in the western part of the island, and particularly in Cambria, or Wales, which is still peopled by their descendants.

Q. What famous British king long resisted the Saxons?

A. Arthur, who was killed in battle, A.D. 542.

Q. What is meant by the Saxon Heptarchy?

A. The word "Heptarchy" means a government of seven kings, and is applied to the seven kingdoms founded by the Saxons in Britain.

Q. Name the seven kingdoms of the Saxon Heptarchy.

A. Kent, Wessex, Northumbria, Sussex, Essex, East Anglia, and Mercia.

Q. Whence did the country receive the name of England?

A. From the Angles, another German nation, who came over with the Saxons.

Q. Who is considered the first king of England?

A. Egbert, King of Wessex, who united in one all the kingdoms of the Heptarchy, and was crowned at Winchester in 827.

Q. When and by whom was Christianity first introduced among the Anglo-Saxons?

A. By St. Augustine, the Apostle of England, who was sent from Rome to this country in 597 by Pope St. Gregory the Great.

Q. What was his success?

A. He converted Ethelbert, King of Kent, became first Archbishop of Canterbury, and he and his followers spread the faith through the other kingdoms of the Heptarchy.

Q. What was Peter's Pence?

A. It was a tax of one penny paid by every Anglo-Saxon to the Holy See.

Q. Mention some of the great ´Anglo - Saxon saints.

A. St. Cuthbert, St. Wilfrid, St. Boniface (Apostle of Germany), and St. Edmund (king and martyr).

Q. Did any men of learning flourish in England at this period?

A. Yes; among others were St. Aldhelm, the Venerable Bede, and Alcuin, the tutor of Charlemagne.

CHAPTER IV.

THE ANGLO-SAXON LINE.   817-1016.

Q. What people first appeared on the coasts of Britain in the reign of Egbert?

A. The Danes, a pagan people from the north of Europe, who lived by piracy.

Q. By whom was Egbert succeeded?

A. By his son Ethelwulf. During his reign and that of his successors England was much harassed by the Danes, who made themselves masters of great part of the kingdom.

Q. What great king successfully resisted the Danes?

A. Alfred the Great, fifth son of Ethelwulf, who became King of England A.D. 872.

Q. Were his first efforts against them successful?

A. No; he was defeated in several engagements, and obliged to retire to the isle of Athelney, in Somersetshire. But after a while he assembled fresh forces, and, after routing the Danes in battle, made peace with them on condition of their embracing Christianity.

Q. Why is he given the surname of Great?

A. On account of his many great actions. For, besides subduing the Danes, he restored learning, founded schools, established a navy and a national militia, made a great number of excellent laws, and governed his people with the greatest prudence and moderation. He was the first to divide England into shires and hundreds.

Q. Who reigned after Alfred?

A. His son Edward the Elder, who was succeeded by his three sons, Athelstan, Edmund I., and Edred, who reigned one after the other.

Q. Did any thing remarkable take place during their reigns?

A. Athelstan, who was a brave and powerful prince, defeated the Danes and Norwegians in a great battle, and had a prosperous reign; his brother Edmund was stabbed at a banquet, by a robber named Leolf; and Edred built the monasteries of Glastonbury, Croyland, and Abingdon.

Q. What great saint was at this time Abbot of Glastonbury?

A. St. Dunstan, afterwards Archbishop of Canterbury, who reformed the clergy, introduced the Benedictine rule into England, acted as chief minister to three kings, and was one of the most learned men of his time.

Q. During whose reigns did St. Dunstan live?

A. During those of Edred, Edwy, and Edgar the Peaceable.

Q. What was the character of these princes?

A. Edwy was a slothful prince, who for his scandalous vices was courageously reproved by St. Dunstan. Edgar was one of the most powerful monarchs of the time. His sovereignty was acknowledged, not only in England, but also in Wales and Ireland; and during his reign the Danes did not dare to attack the land.

Q. What tribute were the Welsh obliged to pay to Edgar ?

A. They paid a tribute of so many wolves' heads ; and thus in a few years England was entirely freed from these animals.

Q. By whom was Edgar succeeded ?

A. By his son St. Edward the Martyr, who was cruelly murdered by his mother-in-law, Queen Elfrida, A.D. 978.

Q. Did the Danes again attack the country ?

A. Yes ; in the reign of Ethelbert II., surnamed the Unready, they renewed their former ravages. Ethelred bribed them to leave the country, and consented to pay them a yearly tribute, which only induced them to return ; so that for many years England was the scene of every sort of misery.

Q. What was the Dane-gelt ?

A. The tax laid on the people for raising the Danish tribute.

Q. What cruel act on the part of Ethelred brought on him the vengeance of the Danes ?

A. A terrible massacre of all the Danes residing in England, which took place by his orders on St. Brice's-day, 1002.

Q. What was the result ?

A. Sweyn, King of Denmark, swore to avenge the deed. He invaded England with a great army, and forced Ethelred to fly to Normandy.

Q. What was the state of England after his death ?

A. His son, Edmund Ironside, a wise and valiant prince, maintained an heroic struggle with the Danes for some years, but was at last treacherously murdered ; and Canute the Great, son of Sweyn, was proclaimed King of England, in the year 1017.

CHAPTER V.

THE DANISH LINE. 1016-1041.

Q. How many Danish kings reigned in England?

A. Three—namely, Canute the Great, Harold I., and Hardicanute.

Q. What was the character of Canute?

A. He was a wise and powerful monarch, and ruled both Danes and English with justice and moderation.

Q. How did he reprove the flattery of his courtiers?

A. Walking one day by the sea-shore at Southampton, his courtiers assured him that he was so powerful a king, that even the sea would obey him, and retire at his word. He commanded a chair to be brought, and, sitting down, commanded the waves to approach no farther.

Q. What was the result?

A. The tide coming in as usual, he bade his courtiers acknowledge their folly and impiety, and keep their homage for Him whom earth and sea obey. Then taking off his crown, he caused it to be hung over the crucifix in Winchester Cathedral, and would never wear it more.

Q. What was the character of Harold and Hardicanute?

A. They were altogether unlike their great father. Hardicanute died from the effects of excessive drinking, A.D. 1041, and with him terminated the Danish line of kings.

CHAPTER VI.

THE SAXON LINE RESTORED. 1041-1066.

Q. Who was chosen king on the death of Hardicanute?

A. Edward, son of Ethelred the Unready, who during the reigns of the Danish kings had lived in exile at the court of Normandy.

Q. By what title is he known in history?

A. He is known as St. Edward the Confessor.

Q. For what is he celebrated?

A. He compiled a famous code of laws, rebuilt Westminster Abbey, and gained the love of his people by his mild government and his many saintly virtues.

Q. What powerful nobleman lived in his reign?

A. Godwin, Earl of Kent, whose daughter Editha was espoused to King Edward.

Q. Who succeeded St. Edward the Confessor?

A. Harold II., the son of Godwin, was raised to the crown; Edgar Atheling, the next heir to St. Edward, being absent from England.

Q. Who was Edgar Atheling?

A. He was grandson to Edmund Ironside, and nephew to St. Edward.

Q. What other prince also claimed the crown?

A. William, Duke of Normandy, who declared that St. Edward had named him his heir, and prepared to invade the kingdom.

Q. Where did he land? and what great battle was fought?

A. Duke William landed with a great army at Pevensey Bay, in Sussex; and shortly after, the battle of Hastings was fought between him and Harold.

Q. What was the result of the battle?

A. Harold was killed, with the flower of the English nobility, and William the Conqueror became King of England. This event is known as the Norman Conquest.

Q. How long had the Saxons reigned in England?

A. More than six hundred years, dating from the time of their first landing.

Q. What had been the general character of the Anglo-Saxons during this period?

A. After their conversion to Christianity, they became a hardy and industrious people, remarkable for their deep religious faith and loyalty to the Holy See. In the earlier period of their history they showed a great love of learning and the arts. Their chief fault was excessive intemperance.

CHAPTER VII.

WILLIAM THE CONQUEROR. 1066-1087.

Q. When was William the Conqueror crowned?

A. On Christmas-day, A.D. 1066.

Q. What was the character of the Conqueror?

A. He was a man of great courage and determined will. He made himself feared and obeyed by his subjects, and ruled with a strong hand. He possessed* great bodily strength, so that it is said no other man could bend his bow or wield his sword.

Q. What were some of the chief events of his reign?

A. He put down an insurrection of the English nobility, and laid waste the whole country between the Humber and the Tyne. He introduced the feudal system into England, compiled Domesday Book, and established the curfew bell. He also fortified the Cinque Ports, built the Tower of London and many other strong castles, instituted the Courts of Exchequer and Chancery, and appointed justices of the peace.

Q. What is meant by the feudal system?

A. The system by which all lands were held on condition of rendering military service to the feudal lord. Thus, the great nobles held their lands as vassals under the crown, their feudal tenants holding lands under them on similar conditions.

Q. What was Domesday Book?

A. A book containing a survey of all the lands in England, with their exact value. It is still preserved.

Q. What was the curfew bell?

A. A bell rung at eight o'clock every evening, as a signal for the putting out of every fire and candle. The object of this was to prevent the English from assembling to concert any plots against their Norman rulers.

Q. Which are the Cinque Ports?

A. Dover, Romney, Hastings, Hythe, and Sandwich.

Q. What great abbey did William found?

A. Battle Abbey, built on the spot where the battle of Hastings was fought.

Q. What oppressive laws did the Conqueror introduce?

A. The forest laws, for preserving game. In order to provide himself with large hunting-grounds, he laid waste sixty villages in Hampshire, and formed what is still called the New Forest.

Q. How many children had he?

A. He had four sons—Robert, Richard, William, and Henry—and five daughters. Robert rebelled against his father, and caused him much trouble.

After his death he succeeded him in the dukedom of Normandy. Richard was gored to death by a stag in the New Forest. William and Henry succeeded one another on the throne of England.

Q. What was the cause of the Conqueror's death?

A. He died from a fall from his horse, while burning the city of Nantes, in France, A.D. 1087.

Q. What was the condition of the English people during his reign?

A. They were terribly oppressed by the Norman nobles, deprived of their lands, and removed from all offices in the state.

Q. What great prelates flourished during his reign?

A. Lanfranc, Archbishop of Canterbury, and St. Osmund, Bishop of Salisbury.

CHAPTER VIII.

WILLIAM II., SURNAMED RUFUS. 1087-1100.

Q. Who succeeded the Conqueror as King of England?

A. His second son, William, surnamed Rufus, from his red hair and complexion.

Q. What was his character?

A. He was a ferocious tyrant, and a cruel oppressor both of his people and of the Church.

Q. What celebrated wars first began in his reign?

A. The Holy Wars, or Crusades, undertaken by the Christian princes and knights of Europe to deliver Jerusalem out of the hands of the infidels. Robert, Duke of Normandy, joined the first Crusade.

Q. What great prelate rebuked William for his crimes, and defended the liberties of the Church?

A. St. Anselm, Archbishop of Canterbury.

c 2

Q. What was the death of William Rufus?

A. He was shot by an arrow whilst hunting in the New Forest.

Q. Who succeeded him?

A. His youngest brother, Henry, seized the crown in the absence of Duke Robert, who had been declared the heir.

CHAPTER IX.

HENRY I., SURNAMED BEAUCLERC, OR THE SCHOLAR.
1100-1135.

Q. What was the charater of Henry I.?

A. He was a brave and learned prince; but cruel, treacherous, and avaricious.

Q. How did he treat his brother Robert?

A. He invaded Normandy, took Robert prisoner, and kept him in captivity during the rest of his life. After the battle of Brenville, 1119, Normandy was added to the English crown. It is said that Henry caused his brother's eyes to be put out in prison.

Q. Whom did Henry marry?

A. Matilda, a Saxon princess. She was daughter to St. Margaret of Scotland, and niece to Edgar Atheling.

Q. Who were his children?

A. Prince William, who died before his father, and Maud, who married, first, Henry V., Emperor of Germany, and secondly, Geoffery Plantagenet, Earl of Anjou.

Q. What was the cause of Prince William's death?

A. He was drowned whilst crossing from Normandy to England in the White ship. His loss so affected King Henry, that it is said he never smiled again.

Q. Who did Henry name to succeed him after the death of the prince?

A. He named as his successor his daughter Maud, to whom all the English and Norman nobles took the oath of allegiance.

Q. What dispute arose between St. Anselm and the king?

A. A dispute concerning investitures, or the right claimed by the king of investing the Bishops with the ring and crosier, the symbols of their spiritual jurisdiction.

Q. Was this claim a lawful one?

A. No; the spiritual jurisdiction belonged, not to the king, but to the Pope.

Q. How did the quarrel terminate?

A. St. Anselm, for his courageous defence of the rights of the Church, was driven into exile; but Henry was at last forced to yield the point.

Q. What custom began in this reign?

A. The custom of using surnames.

Q. What University was founded in England about this time?

A. The University of Cambridge.

Q. When did Henry I. die?

A. He died in 1135, after a reign of thirty-five years. It is said that his death was caused by eating lampreys.

CHAPTER X.

STEPHEN. 1135-1154.

Q. Who succeeded Henry I.?

A. His nephew, Stephen, Earl of Blois.* He had

* He was the son of Stephen, Earl of Blois, and Adela, youngest daughter to William the Conqueror.

sworn allegiance to the Empress Maud, with the rest of the Anglo-Norman nobles ; but on the king's death, he nevertheless seized the crown.

Q. What were the chief events of his reign ?

A. It was entirely taken up with bloody wars between the adherents of Stephen and Maud, in the course of which the country was the scene of great misery.

Q. How did the struggle end ?.

A. It was at last agreed that Stephen should reign over England during his lifetime, but that at his death the crown should descend to Henry Plantagenet, the son of the Empress Maud, who succeeded in maintaining her power in Normandy.

Q. How long did Stephen reign ?

A. Eighteen years. He died in 1154.

CHAPTER XI.

The Line of Plantagenet.

HENRY II. 1154-1189.

Q. Who succeeded Stephen ?

A. Henry II., surnamed Plantagenet, the son of Geoffery Plantagenet, Earl of Anjou, and Maud, daughter to Henry I.

Q. Whom did he marry?

A. He married Eleanor, the heiress of Aquitaine, and through her became sovereign over a large territory in France.

Q. Over what countries did he reign ?

A. Over England and Normandy, inherited from his mother, Anjou from his father, the seven provinces of Aquitaine, brought to him by his wife, and Ireland, which he subdued and added to his dominions in 1171.

Q. What was the character of this monarch?

A. He was one of the most powerful and able monarchs of his time; but he was profligate, tyrannical, and practised in deceit.

Q. What celebrated man became his chief minister?

A. St. Thomas-à-Becket, whom he first made lord chancellor, and afterwards Archbishop of Canterbury.

Q. What course did St. Thomas take on being raised to the dignity of Archbishop?

A. He resigned all his other offices, applied himself wholly to his duties as Primate, and opposed the king's usurpations over the Church with undaunted courage.

Q. How did the struggle between the king and the Archbishop terminate?

A. St. Thomas was driven into exile; but a reconciliation being effected between him and the king after seven years, he returned to his see. Fresh disputes arising between them, however, the king despatched assassins, who murdered the holy Primate before the high altar of his own cathedral, on the 29th of December 1171.

Q. What were the results of this glorious martyrdom?

A. The king was threatened with excommunication; to avoid which terrible sentence he submitted to give up the claims he had unjustly made, and to do public penance at Becket's shrine.

Q. What event brought on a fresh Crusade?

A. The capture of Jerusalem by the Saracens in 1187, which caused a second Crusade to be preached throughout Europe; on which occasion King Henry and many of the English nobility assumed the cross.

Q. Did Henry proceed to the Holy Land?

A. No; he was prevented from doing so by the rebellion of his sons.

Q. How many sons had he?

A. Four—namely, Geoffery, Henry, Richard, and John, the two elder of whom died in their father's lifetime.

Q. In what wars did he engage?

A. Besides the conquest of Ireland, he was engaged in wars with Scotland and France, and frequently with his own rebellious sons and barons.

Q. When and where did he die?

A. He died at Chinon, in Normandy, in 1189, of a broken heart, caused by the ingratitude of his children, and especially of his favourite son John.

Q. What useful changes were introduced in this reign?

A. Trial by jury was established in place of trial by combat. The judges were sent on circuit to administer justice in every part of the kingdom. Charters were granted to the great towns, and some of the more oppressive parts of the feudal system were modified.

Q. What great men flourished in this reign?

A. Nicholas Breakspear, who became Pope under the title of Adrian IV.; Strongbow, Earl of Pembroke, the conqueror of Ireland; St. Thomas of Canterbury; St. Gilbert of Sempringham; and St. Malachi, Archbishop of Armagh.

CHAPTER XII.

RICHARD I., SURNAMED CŒUR-DE-LION.   1189-1199.

Q. Who succeeded Henry II.?

A. His eldest surviving son, Richard, surnamed Cœur-de-Lion, or the Lion-Hearted, from his great personal courage.

Q. What was the character of this prince?

A. He was a man of heroic valour and generosity, handsome in person, and learned for the times ; but passionate, haughty, and headstrong.

Q. What were the chief events of his reign?

A. Immediately after his coronation, he set out for the Holy Land, took the city of Acre, defeated Saladin at the battle of Jaffa, and performed many romantic feats of courage. On his journey homeward he was seized by order of the Duke of Austria and cast into prison, where he was discovered by his faithful minstrel Blondel, and obtained his liberty on payment of a large ransom.

Q. What had taken place in England during his absence?

A. On his return to England he found that his brother John, assisted by the King of France, had rebelled against him. With characteristic generosity, he forgave his brother, and restored him to favour.

Q. How did he die?

A. He was shot with an arrow, whilst besieging the castle of Chaluz, in France, in 1199.

CHAPTER XIII.

JOHN. 1199-1216.

Q. Who succeeded Richard I.?

A. His brother John, to the exclusion of the nearest heir, Arthur, Duke of Brittany.

Q. How was Arthur the nearest heir?

A. He was the son of Geoffery Plantagenet, the eldest son of Henry II.

Q. Did he claim his rights?

A. Yes; he declared war against John, and was supported by the King of France; but was taken prisoner by his uncle, who is generally supposed to have caused him to be secretly murdered.

Q. How did the war with France terminate?

A. By the loss of Normandy, and all King John's French dominions.

Q. What was the character of John?

A. He was the most ruthless tyrant who ever reigned in England, and was equally infamous for cowardice and cruelty.

Q. What were the chief events which made his reign remarkable?

A. On occasion of a dispute regarding the election of Stephen Langton, Archbishop of Canterbury, John banished a great number of ecclesiastics from the kingdom, and seized their revenues. Refusing to receive the Archbishop or to restore the lands, the kingdom was laid under an interdict by Pope Innocent III.

Q. What is an interdict?

A. A sentence by which it is forbidden to celebrate Mass, administer the Sacraments, or perform any other sacred rite.

Q. How long did the interdict last?

A. Six years, at the end of which time John was excommunicated by the Pope. This at last terrified him into submission; and in 1213 Cardinal Pandulph, the Pope's legate, received his oath of fealty to the Holy See, and released the king and his kingdom from the sentences of excommunication and interdict.

Q. What struggle arose between John and his barons?

A. The barons, encouraged by Stephen Langton, demanded of the king a general redress of grievances, and, on the 18th of June 1215, obliged him to sign Magna Charta at Runnymede.

Q. What was Magna Charta?

A. A great Charter, or act, by which all the chief

liberties of the Church and the people were secured to them by the crown, and the most oppressive rights which had been claimed by the Norman kings were solemnly surrendered.

Q. Did John remain faithful to his promise to keep this Charter?

A. Far from it. As soon as he had signed the Charter, he assembled a foreign army, and marched through the land, giving it up to fire and sword.

Q. What did the barons then do?

A. In despair they invited over Louis, Dauphin of France, and offered him the crown. But the further struggle between them was prevented by the death of John, which took place in 1216.

Q. Who succeeded him?

A. His eldest son, Henry of Winchester, who was only ten years old.

CHAPTER XIV.

HENRY III. 1216-1272.

Q. Who governed England during the minority of Henry III.?

A. William, Earl of Pembroke, was chosen Protector. He drove out the French, secured the young king on his throne, caused Magna Charta to be confirmed, and restored peace to the kingdom.

Q. What was the character of King Henry III.?

A. He was pious and charitable, but incapable as a king, and much governed by foreign favourites.

Q. Whom did he marry?

A. Eleanor of Provence.

Q. What were the most remarkable events of his reign?

A. The rebellion of the barons, who elected as

D

their chief Simon de Montfort, Earl of Leicester, and took the government out of the hands of Henry, who, with his son Edward, was defeated at Lewes, and taken prisoner.

Q. What important change was introduced into the Constitution during this time?

A. The counties and boroughs of England were required to send members to represent them in the great Council of the nation, to which none had hitherto been summoned but the great barons. This was the origin of the House of Commons.

Q. Did Henry ever regain his freedom?

A. Yes. In 1265 Prince Edward escaped from prison, defeated De Montfort at Evesham, and restored his father to liberty; after which he set out to join the seventh Crusade.

Q. How long did Henry III. reign?

A. He reigned 56 years, and died in 1272, being buried in Westminster Abbey, which he had rebuilt.

Q. Mention some great men who flourished during his reign.

A. St. Edmund, Archbishop of Canterbury; Grosteste, Bishop of Lincoln; Roger Bacon; Simon de Montfort; and the learned lawyer, Bracton.

Q. Mention some discoveries and inventions introduced at this time.

A. Cider and linen were first made in England; the mariner's compass became known.; and magic-lanterns and magnifying-glasses were invented by Roger Bacon.

CHAPTER XV.

EDWARD I., SURNAMED LONGSHANKS. .1272-1307.

Q. Where was Edward I. at the time of his father's death?

A. He was in the Holy Land, being the last English prince who took part in the Holy Wars.

Q. What was the character and appearance of Edward I.?

A. He was one of the greatest kings who ever reigned in England. He was brave in battle, and wise in council ; but stern, ambitious, and sometimes cruel. In person he was tall and majestic.

Q. What wars did he undertake?

A. He led an army into Wales, and annexed it for ever to the English crown ; after which, he also achieved the conquest of Scotland.

Q. How was the conquest of Scotland brought about?

A. The claim to the Scottish crown being disputed, Edward was chosen as umpire, and decided in favour of John Baliol, whom, however, he first obliged to do homage to him as his liege lord. On Baliol's revolt, Edward marched into Scotland, deposed Baliol, and made himself master of the country.

Q. Did the Scots submit without a struggle?

A. No. Under the brave patriot, William Wallace, they gallantly fought for their independence ; but at length Wallace was taken, carried to London, and executed as a traitor.

Q. Who headed the Scots after the death of Wallace?

A. Robert Bruce, who was crowned King of Scotland. Edward was marching against him with a great army, when he was seized with illness, and died at Carlisle, 1307, in the thirty-fifth year of his reign.

Q. Was his reign remarkable for any thing besides his wars and conquests?

A. Yes. Magna Charta was solemnly confirmed, and a statute was passed forbidding any taxes to be raised without the consent of Parliament. Edward also introduced many valuable improvements into the English laws, which gained him the title of "the English Justinian."

Q. Whom did he marry? and who succeeded him?

A. He was twice married : first to Eleanor of Castile, and secondly to Margaret of France. He was succeeded by his eldest son, Edward of Caernarvon.

Q. What title did this young prince bear?

A. After the conquest of Wales he bore the title of Prince of Wales, which has ever since been conferred on the king's eldest son.

CHAPTER XVI.

EDWARD II. OF CAERNARVON.   1307-1327.

Q. What was the character of Edward II.?

A. He was foolishly attached to favourites, and had none of the great qualities of his father.

Q. What was the first remarkable event of his reign?

A. The total defeat of the English, under their king, at Bannockburn, by the Scots, under Robert Bruce. This victory established the independence of Scotland.

Q. Who was Edward's chief favourite?

A. Piers Gaveston, who was seized and put to death by the barons, headed by the Earl of Lancaster.

Q. Whom did Edward marry?

A. Queen Isabella of France, called for her crimes and cruelty " the She-Wolf of France."

Q. What troubles arose after the death of Gaveston?

A. Edward having chosen Hugh le Despencer for his new favourite, the queen fled to France, in company with a young nobleman named Mortimer ; and returning, with the aid of the discontented barons, raised an army against him, put Despencer to death, deposed the king, and placed his eldest son Edward on the throne.

Q. What was the end of Edward II.?

A. He was cruelly murdered by the queen's orders, in Berkeley Castle, 1327.

CHAPTER XVII.

EDWARD III.   1327-1377.

Q. How old was Edward III. when he was raised to the throne? and to whom was he married?

A. He was just eighteen, and was married to Queen Philippa of Hainault.

Q. Who ruled the kingdom during his minority?

A. His mother Isabella, and her infamous favourite Mortimer ; but Edward seized the latter, and caused him to be executed for his crimes; while Isabella was detained in prison for the rest of her life.

Q. What was the character of Edward III.?

A. He was a truly great prince, brave and chivalrous ; but his ambition engaged him in bloody and unjust wars with France, to the crown of which country he laid claim, in right of his mother.

Q. What were the chief battles fought in the course of these wars?

A. The great battles of Cressy and Poitiers, in which the English totally defeated the French, though the latter were greatly superior to them in numbers.

D 2

and the famous siege of Calais. Edward also gained the naval victory of Sluys.

Q. Who greatly distinguished himself in these wars?

A. Edward the Black Prince, the eldest son of the king, and the most renowned hero of his time.

Q. Was England engaged in any other wars during this reign?

A. Yes; the Scots were defeated, first at Halidon Hill, and afterwards at Neville's Cross; but they succeeded in maintaining their independence.

Q. What two kings were prisoners in England at the same time?

A. John, King of France, taken prisoner at the battle of Poitiers; and David Bruce, King of Scotland, taken at Neville's Cross.

Q. Mention some other remarkable events.

A. The Order of the Garter was instituted, 1350; Windsor Castle was built; the art of weaving cloth introduced into England; gunpowder was invented; and cannon were first used at the battle of Cressy.

Q. Were any improvements introduced into the laws and government?

A. The laws regarding treason were greatly improved; the Commons gained increased liberties and privileges; and a great number of the feudal serfs were set at liberty.

Q. What became of Edward the Black Prince?

A. He undertook an expedition into Spain, to replace Peter the Cruel on the throne of Castile, and gained the great victory of Navaretta; but after this his health broke down, and he died before his father, in 1376.

Q. Was the end of Edward III.'s reign as prosperous as the beginning?

A. No. He lost most of his French conquests;

and at last fell into a state of dotage, and died one year after his son, in 1377, in the fiftieth year of his reign.

Q. Had he any other children?

A. Yes; besides Edward the Black Prince, he had four other sons, from one of whom—Lionel, Duke of Clarence—descended the House of York, and from another—John of Gaunt, Duke of Lancaster—descended the House of Lancaster.

CHAPTER XVIII.

RICHARD II. OF BOURDEAUX.   1377-1399.

Q. By whom was Edward III. succeeded?

A. By his grandson, Richard of Bourdeaux, son of the Black Prince, who was only eleven years of age at the time of his accession.

Q. Who governed the kingdom whilst Richard was a minor?

A. His powerful uncles, the Dukes of Lancaster, York, and Gloucester.

Q. What insurrection broke out in the early part of this reign?

A. The insurrection of the commons, headed by Wat Tyler, who rose to oppose a tax called the poll-tax. A mob of a hundred thousand men assembled on Blackheath, marched to London, and committed many acts of violence.

Q. How was the insurrection quelled?

A. By the presence of mind of the young king, who met the rioters at Smithfield, and induced them to disperse.

Q. What were the other chief events of this reign?

A. During the early part of his reign the king

was deprived of all power by his uncles. At the age
of twenty-two, however, he succeeded in shaking off
their authority, and established a kind of despotism ;
but he was at length deposed by his cousin, Henry of
Lancaster, son of John of Gaunt, who seized the
crown, and forced Richard to abdicate.

Q. What became of Richard ?

A. He was confined a prisoner in Pontefract
Castle, where he was assassinated in 1399.

Q. Whom did he marry ?

A. In 1382 he married Anne of Bohemia, known
as "the good Queen Anne ;" and on her death espoused Isabella of France, by neither of whom did
he leave any children.

Q. Who was the next rightful heir to the throne?

A. Mortimer, Earl of March, from whom the
House of York afterwards descended.

Q. What great man acted as minister to Edward
III. and Richard II. ?

A. William of Wykeham, Bishop of Winchester,
and founder of Winchester School, and New College,
Oxford.

Q. What heresy appeared about this time in
England ?

A. That of John Wycliffe, whose followers were
known as the Lollards.

Q. What poets flourished in England during this
and the following reign ?

A. Chaucer and Gower. The former is called
the " father of English poetry."

Q. What laws were passed in this reign injurious
to the authority of the Holy Roman See ?

A. The Statute of Præmunire, by which it was
forbidden to bring into the country any Papal Bulls,
&c. without permission of the king.

CHAPTER XIX.

Line of Lancaster.

Q. What was the character of Henry IV.?

A. Before his usurpation he had been known as one of the most renowned knights of his time, and was a favourite with the people; but his popularity declined after his accession, and his reign was taken up with plots and insurrections.

Q. Which of these were the most remarkable?

A. That headed by Percy, Earl of Northumberland, and his son Hotspur, assisted by Owen Glendower. They were defeated at Shrewsbury, at which battle Hotspur was slain.

Q. Who was Owen Glendower?

A. He was a Welsh prince, who succeeded in maintaining his independence during the whole of Henry's reign.

Q. What was the character of Henry's eldest son, Henry, Prince of Wales?

A. He caused his father continued trouble by his habits of dissipation, and the unworthy companions with whom he associated ; and on one occasion he was committed to prison by Lord Chief Justice Gascoigne for striking that judge in the open court.

Q. What was the exclamation of the king when he heard of this?

A. "Happy the king who has so courageous a judge, and yet more happy in having a son who will submit to such a punishment!"

Q. What prelate was executed in this reign on a charge of treason?

A. Scroope, Archbishop of York. He was dealt with in so arbitrary a manner that Gascoigne refused to preside at his trial; and the sickness with which Henry was visited during the remainder of his life was regarded by the people as a punishment from God for the death of the Archbishop.

Q. When did Henry die?

A. He died in 1412, leaving four sons; and was succeeded by Henry, Prince of Wales.

CHAPTER XX.

HENRY V. 1413–1422.

Q. How did the young king begin his reign?

A. He dismissed all his worthless companions, and showed himself prepared to govern as became a king.

Q. What insurrection broke out shortly after his accession?

A. An insurrection of the Lollards, headed by Oldcastle, Lord Cobham, who was seized and executed.

Q. In what wars did Henry engage?

A. He revived the old claims of the English kings to the crown of France, and, invading that country, gained the splendid victory of Agincourt in 1415.

Q. What was the result of the war?

A. Henry made himself master of the greater part of France, and the French at last consented to name him heir to the crown and regent of the kingdom, on his marriage with the Princess Catherine, daughter to the reigning king, Charles VI.

Q. Did Henry live to wear the crown of France?

A. No; he died two months before Charles, at the early age of thirty-four.

Q. What was his character?

A. In spite of the wild irregularities of his youth, he showed himself after his accession as wise in council as he was brave in battle. He was the most popular king who ever reigned in England, and administered impartial justice to his people ; but his many great qualities were stained by the boundless ambition which led him into an unjust war of conquest.

CHAPTER XXI.

HENRY VI. 1422-1461.

Q. Who succeeded Henry V. ?

A. His infant son, Henry of Windsor, who was crowned King of England and France, first at Westminster, and the next year at Paris.

Q. Who governed during his minority ?

A. His two uncles, the Dukes of Bedford and Gloucester, the former of whom ruled in France, and the latter in England ; while Cardinal Beaufort, a son of John of Gaunt, and great-uncle to the king, acted as his guardian.

Q. What was the character of Henry VI. ?

A. He was pious and learned, but deficient in the strength of character necessary to control the factions of his fierce nobles. In the sufferings and misfortunes he endured he exhibited the utmost constancy and patience, and he was known by the name of " Holy Henry."

Q. Whom did he marry ?

A. Margaret of Anjou, a woman of masculine courage and energy, by whom he had one son, Prince Edward.

Q. What events took place in France ?

A. On the death of Charles VI., his son assumed the royal title, and recommenced the war. In 1428

a young peasant-girl named Joan of Arc roused the
nation to a more vigorous resistance; and by her
means Charles VII. at last regained possession of his
kingdom, and was crowned at Rheims, the English
being deprived of all their conquests.

Q. What became of Joan of Arc?

A. She was taken prisoner by the English, and
cruelly burnt at Rouen, 1431.

Q. What civil wars broke out during this reign?

A. The bloody Wars of the Roses, waged between
the faction of Richard, Duke of York, who claimed
to be rightful heir to the crown, and the Duke of
Somerset and other supporters of the House of Lancaster.

Q. Why were these wars called the Wars of the
Roses?

A. From the badges worn by the rival parties,—
that of York being a white, and that of Lancaster a
red, rose.

Q. Mention some of the battles fought during
these wars.

A. The battles of St. Alban's and Northampton.
in both of which the king was taken prisoner; the
battle of Wakefield, gained by Queen Margaret, in
which Richard, Duke of York, was slain; the battle of
Mortimer's Cross, gained by Edward, his son, who
assumed the title of king; the bloody battle of Towton,
also gained by Edward and his great partisan the
Earl of Warwick; and the battle of Hexham, which
destroyed the last hopes of the House of Lancaster.

Q. What became of Henry after this battle?

A. He was taken prisoner, and committed to the
Tower of London.

CHAPTER XXII.

Line of York.

EDWARD IV. 1461-1483.

Q. What was the character of Edward IV.?

A. He was brave, and of handsome person, but cruel, profligate, and avaricious.

Q. Did he remain in undisputed possession of the crown?

A. No ; having offended his powerful vassal, the Earl of Warwick, known as the King-maker, that nobleman entered into a negotiation with Queen Margaret, restored King Henry to the throne, and obliged Edward to fly from the kingdom.

Q. What followed this revolution?

A. Edward, having collected troops, returned to England ; Warwick was slain at the battle of Barnet ; Queen Margaret and her son, having risked another battle at Tewkesbury, were entirely defeated, and the young prince cruelly murdered in Edward's presence. Henry was again committed to the Tower, where he also was murdered in 1471, as is supposed, by Richard, Duke of Gloucester.

Q. Whom did Edward marry?

A. Elizabeth Woodville, the widow of a Lancastrian knight. By her he had two sons, Edward and Richard, and four daughters.

Q. What other events marked the reign of Edward IV.?

A. His brother, the Duke of Clarence, was accused of treason, and murdered in the Tower, his body being hidden in a butt of Malmsey wine. The art of printing was brought into England by William Caxton in 1473.

CHAPTER XXIII.

EDWARD V. 1483.

Q. How old was Edward V. at the time of his father's death? and how long did he reign?

A. He was thirteen years of age, and reigned but two months, when his uncle Richard, Duke of Gloucester, seized the crown, and caused the young king and his brother to be smothered in the Tower.

Q. Who was Richard, Duke of Gloucester?

A. He was youngest son of the Duke of York, and brother to King Edward IV.

CHAPTER XXIV.

RICHARD III. 1483-1485.

Q. What was the character of Richard III.?

A. He was the most cruel and treacherous prince of his family, and his ambition led him to the commission of unnumbered crimes. He was possessed, however, of great courage and talents for government.

Q. Whom did he marry?

A. He married Anne Neville, widow to the young Prince Edward, whom he had murdered at Tewkesbury. He is thought to have poisoned her in 1485, in order that he might marry his niece Elizabeth, daughter to Edward IV., and nearest heir to the crown.

Q. How long did he reign?

A. Only two years. In 1485 Henry Tudor, Earl of Richmond, the surviving heir of the house of Lancaster, landed in England, and defeated Richard in the battle of Bosworth. Richard was killed; and his crown, which he wore in the battle, placed on the head of Henry, who was at once proclaimed king.

CHAPTER XXV.

Line of Tudor.

HENRY VII. 1485-1509.

Q. Who was Henry VII.? and whom did he marry?

A. He was the son of Margaret Beaufort, a descendant of John of Gaunt, and Edmund Tudor, Earl of Richmond. He married Elizabeth of York, daughter to Edward IV., by which alliance the houses of York and Lancaster were at last united.

Q. What were the chief events of his reign?

A. The peace of the kingdom was only broken by the rebellions raised by Lambert Simnel and Perkin Warbeck, the latter of whom pretended to be the Duke of York, who had been slain by his uncle in the Tower. After putting down these insurrections, Henry succeeded in breaking up the power of the feudal nobility, and establishing the despotic power of the crown. In this reign America was discovered by Columbus, and commerce was greatly extended.

Q. What children had Henry VII.?

A. He had seven children : his eldest son, Arthur, married to Catherine of Arragon, died before his father, who was succeeded by his next son, Henry ; of his four daughters, Margaret, the eldest, married King James of Scotland, from which marriage were descended the English kings of the House of Stuart.

Q. What was the character of the king?

A. He was crafty and avaricious, but an able and politic ruler. His extortions of money, however, rendered him very unpopular with his subjects. His jealous fear of losing his crown induced him to put to death the young Earl of Warwick, son to George,

Duke of Clarence, and nearest heir of the Plantagenet race. King Henry died in 1509.

CHAPTER XXVI.

HENRY VIII. 1509-1547.

Q. How did Henry VIII. begin his reign?

A. By celebrating his marriage with Catherine of Arragon, his brother's widow, a dispensation for that purpose having been obtained from the Pope.

Q. In what wars did he engage?

A. In a war with France, in which he gained the battle of the Spurs, and one with Scotland, in which James IV. of Scotland was defeated and slain at Flodden Field, 1513.

Q. What celebrated monarchs were reigning at the same time?

A. Charles V., Emperor of Germany ; Francis I., King of France ; and Pope Leo X. Peace was concluded with France in 1519, when the French and English kings met as friends at the celebrated " Field of the Cloth of Gold."

Q. Who was the king's chief minister?

A. Thomas Wolsey, who had risen from a lowly station to the dignities of Cardinal Legate, Archbishop of York, and chancellor of the kingdom. He was a man of great learning and ability, but lost the king's favour, and at last died in disgrace.

Q. What disastrous events took place in this reign ?

A. The religious revolution, known as the Protestant Reformation, began in this reign. It was headed by Martin Luther, a German Augustinian friar, who preached against the authority of the Pope, and denied many of the leading doctrines of the Catholic faith.

Q. Did King Henry at first support the reformers?

A. By no means; he wrote a book against Luther, in defence of the Seven Sacraments, for which he received from the Pope the title of Defender of the Faith.

Q. What events brought on his quarrel with the Holy See?

A. He applied to Rome for a divorce from his queen, Catherine of Arragon, in order that he might marry Anne Boleyn. This not being granted, he separated from the communion of the Holy See, and declared himself supreme head of the Church of England.

Q. Did he divorce his queen?

A. Yes; after which he married Anne Boleyn, but caused her to be beheaded the following year.

Q. How many wives did he successively marry?

A. Six: 1st, Catherine of Arragon, whom he divorced; 2d, Anne Boleyn, who was beheaded; 3d, Jane Seymour, who died in giving birth to a son; 4th, Anne of Cleves, whom he divorced; 5th, Catherine Howard, beheaded; and 6th, Catherine Parr, who survived him.

Q. How many children had he?

A. Three: Mary, daughter to Catherine of Arragon; Elizabeth, daughter to Anne Boleyn; and Edward, son of Jane Seymour.

Q. What steps did the king take after assuming the royal supremacy?

A. He obliged his subjects to acknowledge his supremacy, under pain of death; and he seized all the Church property in England, and suppressed all the abbeys and monasteries, causing a great number of monks to be starved and otherwise put to death.

Q. Did Henry favour the Lutheran doctrines?

E 2

A. By no means : he ordered the heretics to be burnt; whilst the Catholics, who denied his supremacy, were beheaded.

Q. Who were the most famous martyrs put to death for refusing to acknowledge the royal supremacy?

A. Sir Thomas More, chancellor of the kingdom, and Fisher, Bishop of Rochester. A great number of other persons were executed on various pretences. In short, the last years of Henry were truly a reign of terror.

Q. What censure did Pope Paul III. pass on the royal tyrant?

A. He excommunicated him, in 1538.

Q. Who was Henry's chief minister after the death of Wolsey?

A. Thomas Cromwell, Earl of Essex, who, however, lost his favour, and was beheaded.

Q. Who was Archbishop of Canterbury at the same time?

A. Thomas Cranmer, who was a secret Lutheran.

Q. How long did Henry reign?

A. Thirty-eight years. He died in 1547, aged fifty-six, leaving the crown to his son Edward, who was then nine years of age.

CHAPTER XXVII.

EDWARD VI.   1547-1553.

Q. Who governed during the minority of the young king?

A. His uncle, Seymour, Duke of Somerset, was named protector. He was beheaded in 1552, and was succeeded by Dudley, Duke of Northumberland.

Q. What course did Somerset take in affairs of religion?

A. In concert with Cranmer, Archbishop of Canterbury, he abolished the Mass, stripped the churches, introduced the Protestant form of worship, and forced the nation to accept the change.

Q. Was it willingly accepted by the people?

A. Far from it. The people rose in insurrection in all parts to maintain the Catholic religion, but were compelled to submit by foreign troops hired by the protector.

Q. How long did Edward reign?

A. Only six years. Before his death he was persuaded by Northumberland to name as his successor Lady Jane Grey, a descendant of Henry VII., and a Protestant, who had married Lord Guildford Dudley, son to Northumberland.

Q. Why did the Protestant party desire the exclusion of the Princess Mary?

A. Because she remained a zealous Catholic, and refused to give up the Mass.

CHAPTER XXVIII.

MARY I. 1553-1558.

Q. Did the English people side with Mary or with her rival?

A. They warmly supported Mary, who was proclaimed queen; while Lady Jane, her father, and her husband were committed to prison, and afterwards beheaded.

Q. What steps did the new queen take?

A. She restored the Mass, obtained the reconciliation of the country with the Holy See, appointed Catholic Bishops to the various sees, and abolished all her father's cruel statutes of treason.

Q. What rendered her unpopular · with the nation?

A. Her marriage with Philip II., King of Spain, son to the Emperor Charles V.

Q. How were the Protestants treated?

A. They were treated with great severity : as many as two hundred were burnt to death as heretics, including the Protestant Bishops Cranmer, Ridley, and Latimer.

Q. Who were the queen's chief ministers ?

A. Gardiner, Bishop of Winchester, and Cardinal Pole, Archbishop of Canterbury.

Q. What loss did the English sustain during this reign ?

A. The town of Calais was taken by the French. The queen's sorrow at this event is said to have hastened her death.

Q. What was the character of Queen Mary ?

A. She was devoted to the cause of religion, and remarkable for her love of justice and inflexible integrity. She was learned and charitable ; but the religious persecution carried on during her reign has rendered her name odious to Protestant writers.

Q. Who was lawful heir to the crown after the death of Mary?

A. As her sister Elizabeth was not of legitimate birth, the real heir to the crown was Mary Queen of Scots, daughter to James V., and a descendant of Henry VII. But on the promise of Elizabeth to maintain the Catholic faith, Mary consented to name her as her successor.

Q. When did Mary die?

A. In 1558, in the forty-third year of her age.

CHAPTER XXIX.

ELIZABETH.   1558-1602.

Q. What steps did Elizabeth take on succeeding to the crown?

A. She once more assumed the supremacy, restored the Protestant worship, removed the Catholic Bishops and clergy, and prohibited the exercise of the Catholic religion.

Q. Who was her chief minister and her favourite courtier?

A. Cecil, Lord Burleigh, was her minister; but her favourite was Dudley, Earl of Leicester, a man of infamous character.

Q. What was the character of Elizabeth?

A. She was undoubtedly a woman of great talent and power of government; but she was treacherous and tyrannical. Her private life was stained with every vice, and her conduct to Mary Queen of Scots remains a foul blot on her memory.

Q. How did Mary fall into her power?

A. The Scotch Protestants rebelling against their queen, aided and encouraged by Elizabeth, Mary took refuge in England, where she was detained as a prisoner for eighteen years, and finally beheaded, on a pretended charge of treason, in 1506.

Q. What was the real cause of her death?

A. The jealousy of Elizabeth, who feared her as a rival to the throne, and her devoted adherence to the Catholic faith.

Q. How did the English people receive the fresh change of religion?

A. In some parts, especially in the north, they rose in insurrection; and many plots and conspiracies were likewise formed to release Queen Mary.

Q. What was the result of these plots?

A. Their only result was to move the queen and her government to pass the most cruel laws against all who professed the Catholic faith, and refused to acknowledge the royal supremacy.

Q. Were any persons put to death?

A. Upwards of two hundred persons were most savagely executed, solely on the score of religion, and a great number of others on the real or pretended charge of plotting against the queen.

Q. What Pope then filled the chair of St. Peter?

A. St. Pius V., who, in 1570, excommunicated Elizabeth.

Q. Who invaded England in this reign?

A. Philip II. of Spain sent a powerful fleet to invade England. It was known as the Invincible Armada; but it was scattered by a mighty storm, in 1588.

Q. In what other wars did Elizabeth engage?

A. She assisted the Protestants of France and Holland in their rebellions against their rulers; and her naval commanders, Drake and Frobisher, were constantly engaged in attacking the colonies and pillaging the fleets of Spain.

Q. Why is this reign regarded as so glorious by the English people?

A. Chiefly on account of the triumph of the national arms over Spain, the extension of naval and commercial enterprise, and the many great literary men who flourished under Elizabeth.

Q. Who were the most celebrated writers of this age?

A. William Shakespeare, Edmund Spenser, Sir Philip Sidney, and Sir Walter Raleigh.

Q. Who was Elizabeth's favourite after the death of Leicester?

A. The Earl of Essex, whom, however, she caused to be beheaded in 1600.

Q. In what manner did the queen herself die? ·⟩

A. She died, at the age of seventy, a most miserable death, of despair, having filled the throne for forty-five years.

Q. Whom did she name as her successor?

A. She refused to name any one to succeed her; but James VI. of Scotland, son of Mary Queen of Scots, the nearest heir, was acknowledged by the nation, and invited to accept the crown.

Q. What great changes had taken place in the government of England under the Tudor sovereigns?

A. The power of the crown had become despotic, the independence of the parliament was crushed, and the liberties of the subject grossly violated. The encroachments of the royal power were also greatly encouraged by the change of religion, and the new claim put forward of supremacy over the Church.

CHAPTER XXX.

The House of Stuart.

JAMES I. 1603-1625.

Q. What was the character of the new king?

A. He was a man of great learning, but vain and cowardly; given to low and foolish amusements, and particularly to drinking. He was also weakly attached to favourites.

Q. What were the chief events in his reign?

A. Various conspiracies were discovered, for his share in one of which Sir Walter Raleigh was imprisoned, and afterwards beheaded. The Catholics were treated with great severity; and a few of them,

driven to desperation, concerted a plan for blowing
up the Houses of Parliament with gunpowder. This
plot, which was to be executed by Guy Faux, is
known in history as " the Gunpowder Plot."

Q. What was the result of the plot?

A. It was discovered on the 5th of November
1605 ; all those concerned in it were seized and put
to death, and fresh laws of great cruelty were in consequence passed against the whole Catholic body.

Q. Who were the Missionary Priests ?

A. They were English priests sent into England
from foreign countries to administer to the spiritual
wants of the English Catholics, at the peril of their
lives ; the punishment of death being decreed to all
priests found in the kingdom.

Q. Were many put to death?

A. Eighteen priests were executed during the
reign of James solely for their priestly character, and
a great number of others suffered on the charge of
being concerned in the Gunpowder Plot.

Q. Whom did James marry? and who were his
children?

A. He married Anne of Denmark. His eldest
son, Henry, died in 1612. His other children were—
Charles, who succeeded him, and Elizabeth, who
married the Elector of Bavaria, from whom our
present royal family is descended.

Q. What celebrated man was chancellor in this
reign?

A. Francis, Lord Bacon, one of the greatest of
English philosophers ; who, however, was disgraced
and deprived of his office on the charge of accepting
bribes.

CHAPTER XXXI.

CHARLES I. 1625-1649.

Q. What was the character of Charles I.?

A. He was a man of sincere piety and domestic virtue, but fond of arbitrary power, and too often insincere in his dealings with his subjects. He had a kingly and commanding person, and a cultivated mind. The patience and dignity which he exhibited under misfortune were truly worthy of our admiration.

Q. In what difficulties was he involved at his accession?

A. He found the nation engaged in war with Spain and Austria; but on applying to his parliament for money to carry on these wars, they refused him supplies, and demanded a redress of grievances.

Q. How did the king act?

A. He dissolved the parliament, and endeavoured to raise money by his own authority, without the consent of parliament.

Q. Who were his favourite ministers?

A. First, George Villiers, Duke of Buckingham, who was assassinated in 1628; and afterwards Wentworth, Earl of Strafford, a man of great talent and determination, who endeavoured to render his master's power despotic both in England and Ireland; and William Laud, Archbishop of Canterbury.

Q. What great petition was presented to the king in 1628?

A. The Petition of Rights, which demanded the restoration of all the ancient liberties of the people.

Q. Who were the Puritans?

A. They were the extreme Protestants, who desired to abolish the government of Bishops, and accused the king of favouring Popery because he would not enforce the cruel penal laws against Catholics. They were also supporters of the popular cause.

Q. Who were the chief leaders of the popular party?

A. Pym, Vane, and Hampden.

Q. How did Hampden first become celebrated?

A. By opposing the tax called Ship-money, which was raised by the king's authority for the support of the navy.

Q. Who were the Scottish Covenanters?

A. Those who took up arms to resist the government of Bishops, and the introduction into Scotland of the English Prayer-book.

Q. What was the consequence of the rebellion in Scotland?

A. Charles was obliged to call a parliament, to put down the rebellion.

Q. What was this parliament called? and how did it act?

A. It is known as the Long Parliament; and instead of granting supplies, the members proceeded to impeach of treason Laud and Strafford, both of whom were beheaded.

Q. What brought on the final rupture between the king and parliament?

A. An attempt on the part of the king to arrest the five leading members of the House of Commons.

Q. When and where was the first engagement fought?

A. At Edgehill, in Warwickshire, in 1642, where both parties claimed the victory.

Q. What names were conferred on the supporters of the king and of the parliament?

A. The former were known as Cavaliers; the latter as Roundheads.

Q. Mention some of the most famous Cavaliers.

A. Prince Rupert, nephew to the king, Lord Falkland, and the Marquis of Montrose.

Q. Who were the chief parliamentary leaders?

A. The Earl of Essex, Lord Fairfax, and Oliver Cromwell.

Q. Which were the two greatest victories gained by Cromwell?

A. The battles of Marston Moor and Naseby.

Q. What became of Charles after the battle of Naseby?

A. He was forced to break up his army, and in 1647 fled to the Scottish camp; but the Scottish leaders sold him to the English parliament for the sum of 400,000*l.*

Q. How did they treat him?

A. After imprisoning him in various places, he was at last, through the intrigues of Cromwell, brought to trial before the Commons, in Westminster Hall, on the charge of high treason, and condemned to death.

Q. When and where was this sentence executed?

A. Before the royal palace of Whitehall, where King Charles was beheaded, on the 30th of January 1649.

Q. How did the king behave at his trial and execution?

A. He showed the utmost dignity, fortitude, and patience.

Q. What was the general feeling of the country on this event?

A. It filled all ranks with pity and admiration for the unfortunate king, and horror at the crime of his murderers.

Q. Whom did Charles I. marry?

A. Henrietta Maria, daughter of Henry IV. of

France, by whom he had three sons and three daughters.

_____

CHAPTER XXXII.

THE COMMONWEALTH AND OLIVER CROMWELL. 1649-1660.

Q. What form of government was established after the death of Charles ?

A. A republic, or commonwealth, the chief power being in the hands of Cromwell, who, in 1653, was named lord protector.

Q. Did the Scotch acknowledge the new government?

A. No. They proclaimed Charles, Prince of Wales, king, in room of his father.   .

Q. In what battles did Cromwell defeat the Scottish and English royalists ? .

A. In the battles of Dunbar and Worcester.

Q. What became of Charles II. after the battle of Worcester ?

A. He was obliged to fly; and, after the most romantic adventures, escaped to Holland.

Q. Was the struggle likewise carried on in Ireland ?

A. Yes ; but the country was reduced to submission by Cromwell, after a bloody campaign, in which the most atrocious cruelties were perpetrated by the English troops.

Q. Mention some of the chief acts of Cromwell's government.

A. He dissolved the Long Parliament in 1653, declared war against Spain and Holland, and governed for five years with great prudence and vigour.

Q. What victories were gained over the Dutch and Spaniards ?

A. The Dutch fleet was defeated by Admiral Blake, Jamaica was taken from the Spaniards, and the town of Dunkirk surrendered to England in 1658.

Q. What was the character of Cromwell?

A. He was a man of extraordinary talent, both in government and military command; but his character is odious for its dissimulation and hypocrisy.

Q. What celebrated man acted as Latin secretary to Cromwell?

A. John Milton, author of the *Paradise Lost,* one of the greatest poets of the English nation.

Q. What religious changes took place under the Commonwealth?

A. The Protestant episcopacy and Anglican Prayer-book were abolished, and Catholics were exposed to severe persecution.

Q. When did Cromwell die? and who succeeded him in the government?

A. He died on the 3d of September 1658, when his son Richard was proclaimed protector; but he soon resigned this dignity.

Q. Who at last brought about the restoration of the monarchy?

A. General Monk, who called a fresh parliament, by whom it was resolved to invite Charles II. to return to his kingdom.

CHAPTER XXXIII.

CHARLES II. 1660-1685.

Q. How was the king's return welcomed by his people?

A. It was welcomed with universal joy by the whole nation.

Q. What was the character of the new king?

A. He was witty and good-natured, but indolent, and abandoned to unworthy pleasures.

Q. In what wars did England engage during his reign?

A. In bloody naval wars with the Dutch, in the course of which the Dutch entered the Medway and burnt the English shipping. The English, however, gained several splendid victories, and the struggle ended by establishing the naval supremacy of this country.

Q. What great calamities marked this reign?

A. In 1665 the plague broke out in London, and carried off 100,000 persons ; and in the following year occurred the great fire of London, which burned down 13,000 houses and 90 churches.

Q. What celebrated Acts of Parliament were passed in this reign?

A. The Test and Corporation Acts, which excluded Catholics from parliament, as well as from holding any office in the State, and the Habeas Corpus Act, which provided for the personal liberty of the subject.

Q. Who was the chief leader of the agitation against Catholics?

A. Ashley, Lord Shaftesbury, who sought to win popularity by exciting the bigotry of the nation against the Catholics.

Q. What was the Popish Plot?

A. A supposed plot, which Shaftesbury and his party pretended to have been framed by the Catholics for the murder of the king and the destruction of the metropolis.

Q. Who was the witness who swore to this plot?

A. Titus Oates, a man of infamous character, on whose evidence many Catholics were put to death.

Q. What political parties date their origin from the reign of Charles II.?

A. The Whigs and Tories.

Q. What was the chief object of the Whigs?

A. Their chief object was to exclude James, Duke of York, brother to the king, from succeeding him on the throne, that prince having embraced the Catholic faith.

Q. Who were the principal Whig leaders?

A. Lord William Russell and Algernon Sidney.

Q. What was the Rye-House Plot?

A. A treasonable conspiracy, in which many of the Whig party engaged on the failure of their schemes for the exclusion of James. In consequence of their share in this plot, Russell and Sidney were executed as traitors, in 1683.

Q. What was the state of society during this reign?

A. It was marked by the general spread of irreligion and profligacy.

Q. When did Charles II. die?

A. He died in 1685, having before his death been secretly reconciled to the Catholic Church.

Q. Whom did he marry?

A. He married Catherine of Braganza ; but having no children by her, the crown passed to his brother, James, Duke of York.

CHAPTER XXXIV.

JAMES II. 1685-1688.

Q. What was the character of James II.?

A. In the earlier part of his life he had distinguished himself for his bravery and skill as a naval commander ; he was honest and upright in his pub-

lic conduct ; but obstinate, and attached to arbitrary
power ; and his religion rendered him unpopular with
the nation at large.

Q. What rebellion broke out soon after his accession ?

A. An insurrection headed by the Duke of Mon-
mouth, a natural son of the late king, who was taken
prisoner at Sedgmoor, and executed as a traitor.

Q. What measures did the king take which roused
the opposition of the popular party?

A. He published a declaration dispensing with the
oaths which excluded Catholics from holding State
offices, and ordered it to be read in all churches.
Seven of the Protestant Bishops protesting against this
act were sent to the Tower, but acquitted on their
trial.

Q. Had James any children ?

A. By his first wife, Anne Hyde, he had two
daughters (both educated as Protestants), Mary and
Anne, the first of whom was married to William,
Prince of Orange, and was regarded as heir to the
throne. But in 1688 his second wife, Mary Beatrice,
of Modena, gave birth to a son, James Francis Edward, who was brought up in the Catholic faith.

Q. What steps did the Whig nobles resolve on,
in order to resist the arbitrary measures of the king,
and exclude his son from the throne ?

A. They invited William of Orange over to England in 1688, and offered him the crown.

Q. What part did the two daughters of James take
in this revolution ?

A. They took an active part against their unfortunate father, who was obliged to fly to France, and
was declared to have abdicated the crown.

CHAPTER XXXV.

WILLIAM AND MARY. 1688-1702.

Q. What government was established after the light of James ?

A. A Convention Parliament settled the crown ointly on William of Orange and the Princess Mary, iis wife.

Q. Was this change desired by the great mass of he people ?

A. It appears certain that the majority of the people were in favour of King James, and that the ·evolution was entirely the work of a small but power-'ul faction of Whig nobles.

Q. What important measure was passed by the Convention Parliament?

A. The Bill of Rights, which deprived the crown)f all absolute power, and declared that no Catholic hould thenceforth be allowed to succeed to the throne.

Q. How was the revolution received in Scotland ?

A. The standard of King James was raised by he brave Viscount Dundee, who was killed at Killie-rankie in the moment of victory. After his death, he cause of James was lost for want of a leader.

Q. Did James take no steps himself to defend his ·ights ?

A. Supported by the King of France, he landed n Ireland, where the people had refused to acknow-edge the authority of William ; but was totally de-eated by his son-in-law at the battle of the Boyne, ind forced to return to France.

Q. Was any other battle fought between the two)arties ?

A. Several naval battles were fought ; but in 692 the English and Dutch gained a decisive victory over the French off Cape La Hogue, which entirely deprived James of all hopes of recovering his kingdom.

Q. In what wars was William engaged during his reign ?

A. In long wars with Louis XIV., King of France, in the course of which he sustained repeated defeats.

Q. Mention some other remarkable events of his reign.

A. The Bank of England was founded, 1691; the Toleration Act passed, for relieving all sects of Protestant Dissenters; and the Act of Succession passed in 1700, whereby the crown was settled on the Princess Anne, and, after her death without children, on the Protestant descendants of King James I.

Q. In what scheme was William engaged at the time of his death ?

A. In a scheme for uniting all the powers of Europe in an alliance against France.

Q. What was the object of this alliance ?

A. To prevent the succession to the crown of Spain from passing to the grandson of Louis XIV.

Q. When did William die ?

A. He died from a fall from his horse, in 1702. Queen Mary died six years previously, leaving no children ; the crown, therefore, passed to her sister, the Princess Anne. The death of King James took place a few months before that of William.

Q. What was the character of William III.?

A. He was cold and unamiable, but was reputed one of the greatest generals of his time.

CHAPTER XXXVI.

QUEEN ANNE. 1702-1715.

Q. What war broke out immediately on the accession of Anne ?

A. That known as the "War of the Spanish Succession," in which England, Holland, and the Empire were allied against France.

Q. What step had Louis XIV. taken offensive to the English Government ?

A. He had acknowledged the young Prince James Francis King of England on the death of his father, James II.

Q. How was this prince known in England ?

A. By the name of the Pretender.

Q. What name was given to his supporters in England ?

A. They were called Jacobites.

Q. To whom was Queen Anne married ?

A. To Prince George of Denmark, by whom she had seventeen children, all of whom died in infancy.

Q. What was her character ?

A. She was kind-hearted, and popular with her subjects, though coarse in her manners, and deficient in education. Her chief fault was her undutiful conduct to her father, of which, however, she appears to have bitterly repented.

Q. Who was her great general, and what victories did he gain over the French ?

A. Churchill, Duke of Marlborough, who gained the great victory of Blenheim in 1704, and those of Ramilies, Oudenarde, and Malplaquet in the following years.

Q. What other success was obtained by the British arms?

A. The strong tower of Gibraltar was captured by Sir George Rooke in 1704.

Q. What other memorable event took place in this reign?

A. The union between England and Scotland took place in 1707.

Q. For what else was the reign of Anne remarkable?

A. For the number of distinguished literary men who flourished at this time, among whom were Pope, Swift, Steele, Addison, and Sir Isaac Newton.

Q. What was the state of politics in this reign?

A. A fierce struggle was kept up between the Whigs, who supported the principles of the Revolution, and the Tories, who were most of them Jacobites.

Q. From what party did the queen choose her ministers?

A. During the greater part of her reign she was forced to accept a Whig ministry, who aimed at maintaining the war with France. But in 1713 the Whigs were driven from power, and succeeded by a Tory ministry, headed by Harley, Earl of Oxford, and Lord Bolingbroke.

Q. By whom was the queen chiefly governed?

A. By Sarah, the celebrated Duchess of Marlborough, whose disgrace at last brought about the fall of the Whigs.

Q. How long did the "War of the Spanish Succession" last?

A. It lasted for eleven years, from 1702 to 1713, when the Peace of Utrecht put an end to further hostilities.

Q. What scheme was entertained by Harley and Bolingbroke?

A. They secretly schemed at securing the succession of the throne to the exiled Prince James Francis;

but the death of the queen taking place in 1714, before their plans were matured, George, Elector of Hanover, was at once proclaimed king, according to the provisions of the Act of Succession.

CHAPTER XXXVII.

House of Brunswick.

GEORGE I. 1715-1727.

Q. Who was George I.?

A. He was grandson of Elizabeth, Queen of Bohemia, daughter to King James I., and was the nearest Protestant heir to the crown, all the surviving descendants of Charles I. having become Catholics.

Q. What was his character?

A. He had the reputation of being brave in battle; but his manners were gross and licentious, and avarice was his ruling passion.

Q. What events followed on his accession?

A. The Tory ministers of Queen Anne were impeached for high treason, and committed to the Tower; and in the following year, 1715, the standard of the Pretender was raised in Scotland by the Earl of Mar, and in England by the Earl of Derwentwater, whose forces were, however, defeated, and the rebellion soon extinguished.

Q. What became of the Jacobite leaders?

A. Lord Derwentwater and some others were taken prisoners, and executed as traitors.

Q. Who was the chief minister of George I.?

A. Sir Robert Walpole, who held office under him and his successor for twenty-three years.

Q. Mention some other events of this reign.

A. In 1718 the Quadruple Alliance was signed

G

between England, Holland, France, and the Empire, and war broke out with Spain. In 1718 the South-Sea Bubble, a scheme of wild speculation, ruined many thousand families, and nearly brought on a national bankruptcy. In 1722 rumours arose of fresh Jacobite conspiracies ; Atterbury, Bishop of Rochester, was banished, and severe laws passed against the Catholics.

Q. When did George I. die ?

A. He died at Osnaburg in 1727, leaving the crown to his son, George, Prince of Wales, with whom he had been on bad terms for many years.

CHAPTER XXXVIII.

GEORGE II.   1727-1760.

Q. What was the character of George II. ?

A. He was of sullen temper and profligate life. He was wholly illiterate, and, like his father, showed a marked preference for his Hanoverian over his English subjects. He was, however, distinguished for personal bravery.

Q. Whom did he marry ?

A. Caroline of Anspach, a princess of some character for learning.

Q. What wars were carried on in this reign ?

A. A war with Spain broke out in 1737, in which England gained but little advantage. In 1742 this country became involved in a continental war, in support of Austria against France and Prussia.

Q. What battles were fought in this war ?

A. The battle of Dettingen, gained by the English, and the last in which an English king ever commanded in person ; and the battle of Fontenoy, in which the English, under the Duke of Cumberland, were totally defeated. This war was terminated in 1743 by the Peace of Aix-la-Chapelle.

Q. What insurrection broke out in 1745?

A. Prince Charles Edward Stuart, commonly called the Young Pretender, son to James Francis, landed in Scotland, and raised the Highland clans.

Q. Did he meet with any success?

A. He marched to Edinburgh, and defeated the king's troops at Preston Pans and Falkirk, and advanced into England as far as Derby ; but returning to Scotland, was attacked at Culloden Moor by the Duke of Cumberland, where his little army was totally defeated.

Q. How were the Jacobites treated after this insurrection?

A. The victory of Culloden was followed up with barbarous executions, and military law proclaimed throughout the Highlands.

Q. What became of Prince Charles Edward?

A. After concealing himself for five months in the Highlands, he at last succeeded in escaping to France.

Q. What was the " Seven Years' War"?

A. A war between France and England, in which the latter country engaged in order to defend the king's Hanoverian States, and which at first proved very disastrous to the English arms.

Q. What great minister retrieved the honour of the country?

A. Pitt, afterwards Earl of Chatham, under whose government Canada was conquered by General Wolfe, several great naval victories were gained, and the foundation of our Indian empire was laid by the conquests of the great Lord Clive.

Q. How long did George II. reign?

A. He reigned thirty-three years, and expired

suddenly in 1760. His eldest son, Frederick, Prince of Wales, having died in his father's lifetime, the crown passed to the son of that prince, who accordingly succeeded his grandfather, under the title of George III.

CHAPTER XXXIX.

GEORGE III. 1760-1820.

Q. What was the age of the young monarch, and whom did he marry?

A. He was just twenty-two when he became king, and the following year he married Charlotte of Mecklenburg, by whom he had fifteen children.

Q. Did the war with France continue under the new reign?

A. It continued for three years, but was brought to a close in 1763 by the Peace of Paris, many important colonial possessions being secured to Great Britain.

Q. What was the first important event in the reign of George III.?

A. The rupture between Great Britain and her North-American colonies, which ended in the latter obtaining their independence.

Q. What was the cause of this rupture?

A. The arbitrary measures of the British ministers, who claimed to lay taxes on the Americans for the support of the home government.

Q. Who was the leader of the American armies?

A. George Washington, a man of great ability and virtue.

Q. What events took place in the course of the war?

A. The English arms met with great disasters—

two English armies were forced to surrender to the enemy; and in 1778 France took part with America, and war broke out with that country and also with Spain.

Q. When was the independence of the United States at last acknowledged by Great Britain?

A. In 1783, when a treaty of peace was signed at Versailles.

Q. What celebrated riots took place in London in 1780?

A. Those known as the "No-Popery" riots, in the course of which a great number of Catholic chapels were burnt by the mob, and frightful excesses were committed. The instigator of these riots was Lord George Gordon.

Q. What events took place in France in 1789?

A. A great revolution broke out, in the course of which, after terrible scenes of violence and bloodshed, the king, Louis XVI., and his queen, with a great number of persons of every rank, were brought to the scaffold.

Q. What minister was at the head of the English Government at this time?

A. William Pitt, son of the great Earl of Chatham.

Q. When did war commence between France and England, and with what result?

A. War was declared in 1793; and though unsuccessful on land, the English gained several splendid naval victories under her Admirals Howe, Jervis, Duncan, and Nelson.

Q. What rebellion threatened to disturb the interior tranquillity of the kingdom?

A. A rebellion in Ireland, the inhabitants of which country suffered great hardships. The rebellion was, however, soon repressed; and in 1800 the union

between Great Britain and Ireland was effected, in
spite of the general discontent of the Irish people.

Q. What great victory was gained in 1798 by
Lord Nelson ?

A. The great battle of the Nile, in which the
French fleet was almost entirely destroyed.

Q. What great man was placed at this time at
the head of the French Republic ?

A. Napoleon Bonaparte, a Corsican by birth,
who in 1799 became first consul.

Q. When did the war terminate ?

A. In 1802 the Treaty of Amiens was signed,
which was followed by a short interval of peace ; but
in the following year hostilities between the two
countries were renewed, and Napoleon, who in 1804
assumed the title of emperor, prepared an army for
the invasion of England.

Q. What prevented the execution of this design ?

A. The great naval victory of Trafalgar, gained
by Lord Nelson over the combined fleets of France
and Spain in 1805, in which, however, the English
lost their heroic commander.

Q. Did the other European States join in the
war ?

A. Yes ; Austria, Russia, and Prussia all joined
in alliance with England against France ; but the
repeated victories of Napoleon compelled these powers
to come to terms of peace, which left the French emperor virtually master of Europe.

Q. What events of domestic interest had mean-
while taken place in England ?

A. A great number of Catholic priests and religious communities took refuge in England at the
outburst of the French Revolution, and were received
with generous hospitality. An agitation was set on
foot for the repeal of the oppressive penal laws against

Catholics, and measures of relief were proposed ; but failed, in consequence of the king's opposition. Pitt, the first minister of the crown, died in 1806 ; and in 1811, the king being attacked with insanity, his eldest son, George, Prince of Wales, was appointed regent.

Q. What gave rise to the Peninsular war ?

A. Napoleon having dethroned the royal family of Spain, and given the crown to his brother Joseph, the Spanish people rose in insurrection, and implored the help of England.

Q. What general commanded the English army in the Peninsula?

A. Sir Arthur Wellesley, afterwards Duke of Wellington.

Q. Name his chief victories over the French.

A. He gained the victories of Vimiera, the Douro, Talavera, Salamanca, and Vittoria, and in 1814 drove the French across the Pyrenees, and defeated Marshal Soult at the battle of Toulouse.

Q. What brought on the fall of Napoleon ?

A. In 1812 he led a great expedition into the heart of Russia, but was forced to retreat in the depth of winter, and his immense army perished.

Q. What followed on this disaster ?

A. Austria and Prussia once more declared war ; in 1814 the armies of the allies occupied Paris ; Napoleon was forced to abdicate, and retire to the isle of Elba; and the Bourbons were restored to the throne of France.

Q. What took place on the declaration of peace ?

A. The sovereigns of Russia, Austria, and Prussia visited England, and were entertained by the prince regent with great splendour ; and a congress met at Vienna to restore to the different States of Europe their former territories.

Q. Was the peace of long duration ?

A. No. In 1815 Napoleon quitted Elba, landed in France, and once more seized the throne.

Q. Where did he receive his final overthrow?

A. At the battle of Waterloo, where he was totally defeated by the English and Prussians, under the Duke of Wellington, June 18th, 1815.

Q. What became of him after this defeat?

A. He surrendered to the English, and was sent prisoner to the island of St. Helena, where he died in 1821.

Q. What other events took place during the long reign of George III.?

A. A brief war broke out with America in 1812. Algiers was bombarded by Lord Exmouth in 1816. The slave-trade was abolished in 1807. Gas began to be used in 1802; and an immense impulse was given to the cotton manufacture, by improvements in the steam-engine, introduced by James Watt.

Q. Mention some of the great men who flourished in this reign.

A. Fox, Burke, and Sheridan (orators); Dr. Johnson and Oliver Goldsmith (prose writers); Scott, Wordsworth, Coleridge, and Byron (poets); Lords Hill and Beresford, Sir Ralph Abercrombie, and Sir Sidney Smith (military commanders); John Howard, the philanthropist, and the reformer of prison discipline.

Q. When did the king die, and what was his character?

A. He died in 1820, at the age of eighty-two, having reigned sixty years. He was a man of sincere piety and integrity of character, and universally respected for his goodness of heart.

CHAPTER XL.

GEORGE IV. 1820-1830.

Q. By whom was George III. succeeded?

A. By his eldest son, George, Prince of Wales.

Q. To whom was he married?

A. To his cousin, Caroline of Brunswick, by whom he had one daughter, the Princess Charlotte, who, to the great regret of the nation, died in 1817.

Q. What was the character of the new king?

A. He was graceful in manners and appearance, but selfish, dissipated, and extravagant, and most unpopular with the nation.

Q. What conspiracy was discovered in the beginning of his reign?

A. The Cato-Street conspiracy, the object of which was to assassinate the king's ministers.

Q. What gave rise to this conspiracy?

A. The great distress of the lower orders, and the arbitrary measures of Lord Castlereagh and other ministers of the crown.

Q. What further increased the unpopularity of the king?

A. His conduct to his wife, whom he refused to be allowed to be crowned as queen, and against whom a bill of pains and penalties was introduced into parliament, depriving her of her rank and dignities, on certain charges brought against her.

Q. What question caused great agitation in Ireland?

A. The question of Catholic Emancipation, to carry which the Catholic Association was formed by Daniel O'Connell.

Q. What celebrated statesman supported the Catholic claims?

A. George Canning, who became prime minister in 1827, but died shortly afterwards.

Q. When was Catholic Emancipation at last granted?

A. In 1829, under the ministry of the Duke of Wellington and Sir Robert Peel, when a bill was passed by which Catholics were allowed to sit in parliament, and hold commissions in the army and navy.

Q. When did the king die? and by whom was he succeeded?

A. He died in 1830, and was succeeded by his eldest surviving brother, William, Duke of Clarence.

———

CHAPTER XLI.

WILLIAM IV.　1830-1837.

Q. What events of importance took place in the beginning of this reign?

A. A fresh revolution broke out in France; King Charles X. was dethroned, and took refuge in England; and Louis Philippe, Duke of Orleans, was declared King of the French.

Q. What caused great popular excitement in England?

A. The question of Parliamentary Reform, which was generally demanded by the people, but resisted by the House of Lords.

Q. When was the Reform Bill at last passed? and what changes did it introduce?

A. It was passed in 1832, under the ministry of Earl Grey. By its provisions the franchise was considerably extended, and many large towns represented in parliament.

Q. To whom was the king married?

A. To Queen Adelaide of Saxe Meinengen, by whom he had no children.

Q. What was his character?

A. He was frank and good-natured, had distinguished himself in early life as a brave sailor, and enjoyed considerable popularity.

Q. When did he die?

A. In 1837; and, leaving no issue, was succeeded by the Princess Victoria, daughter to his next brother, Edward, Duke of Kent.

CHAPTER XLII.

VICTORIA. 1837.

Q. What age was the young queen? and whom did she marry?

A. She was just eighteen when she ascended the throne; and in 1840 she married her cousin, Prince Albert of Saxe Coburg, who died, much regretted, in 1862.

Q. In what wars has England been engaged during the present reign?

A. In a war in Syria with the Pacha of Egypt, 1840; another in Affghanistan, 1841; in China, 1842; and in India, 1849, which ended in the conquest of Scinde and the Punjaub. Rebellions likewise broke out in Canada and Ireland.

Q. What European war broke out in 1854?

A. One with Russia, in which France and England formed an alliance to protect Turkey; and the allied armies proceeded to the Crimea, and laid siege to Sebastopol.

Q. What battles were fought in the Crimean war?

A. The battles of the Alma, Balaklava, and Ink-erman. In 1855 Sebastopol was taken, and peace was restored the following year.

Q. What insurrection broke out in 1857?

A. An insurrection of the native troops employed in India, which was put down after much bloodshed.

Q. What event took place in 1850 affecting the Catholics of England?

A. Pope Pius IX. restored the English hierarchy of Bishops, erecting one archbishopric and twelve bishoprics. This step caused much excitement in the country.

Q. What inventions have signalised this reign?

A. Railways and steam-navigation have greatly increased. The electric telegraph was first worked in 1842. The system of penny postage was intro-duced by Sir Rowland Hill in 1840. Two Exhibi-tions of the industry of all nations have taken place in London—one in 1851, and another in 1862.

Q. What event of domestic interest took place in 1863?

A. The marriage of Albert Edward, Prince of Wales, to the Princess Alexandra of Denmark.

THE END.